The Goodnight Caterpillar
A Children's Relaxation Story

Lori Lite

Illustrated by Kimberly C. Fox

Stress Free Kids

I dedicate this book

to my husband

who keeps my dreams alive.

He believes with all his heart and soul

that my books can change the world.

His belief fills me with

the light of hope

and the confidence I need

to inspire others to find their answers.

Collect the Indigo Dreams Series and watch your whole family manage anxiety, stress and anger...

CD/Audio Books:

Indigo Dreams

Indigo Ocean Dreams

Indigo Teen Dreams

*Indigo Dreams:
Garden of Wellness*

*Indigo Dreams:
Adult Relaxation*

*Indigo Dreams:
3 CD Set*

Books:

The Goodnight Caterpillar

A Boy and a Turtle

Bubble Riding

Angry Octopus

Sea Otter Cove

Affirmation Weaver

A Boy and a Bear

The Affirmation Web

Curriculum Kits:

Children's Wellness Curriculum

Children's Stress Awareness Curriculum

**Books, CDs, curriculums, and other products designed
to empower children, teens, and adults are available at
www.StressFreeKids.com**

Congratulations!

You have taken a wonderful step in bringing relaxation to your child.

The Goodnight Caterpillar is designed to relax your child's mind and body, and prepare them for the best sleep ever. Both you and your child will learn to send a relaxation signal to every part of your body. Children easily follow the animated caterpillar along as he learns to "slow down, relax, and even see things more clearly."

Step by step, both parent and child learn a simple relaxation technique that will help manage stress and improve sleep.

My own children know to ask for *the caterpillar story* during restless moments. It is a thrill for me to watch them fall asleep during this story. I invite you, as well, to treat yourself to this technique and enjoy falling asleep peacefully.

Lori Lite

A child sat in a meadow.

The fragrance of wildflowers encircled her head

and the gentle breeze embraced her.

The sun's warm rays danced upon her face.

A rustling in the grass awakened the girl from her quiet moment.

A caterpillar, tied up in knots, tumbled out from beneath her.

"Why are you in knots?" asked the child.

The caterpillar answered in a rushed voice. "I'm all in knots because I'm very uptight and I'm in a very big hurry."

"My goodness! Why are you in such a hurry?"

"I have to hurry," the caterpillar answered.

"I have to find lots of leaves to eat.

I have to eat them quickly so that I can

grow big enough to spin a cocoon.

I have to search and find the perfect spot to build

my cocoon. Once I do that my work really begins.

I have to spin myself a cocoon, all before the sun goes down."

The child giggled and said, "Just close your eyes and take a deep breath. I will show you how to slow down, relax, and even see things more clearly."

With a steady, soothing voice, the child spoke these words. "You are going to relax your feet. You will relax your feet. Your feet are relaxing. Your feet are relaxed."

Surprisingly enough, all of the caterpillar's feet relaxed.

The child continued.

"You are going to relax your legs.

You will relax your legs. Your legs are relaxing.

Your legs are relaxed."

The caterpillar's legs dropped gently toward the welcoming earth.

The child took a deep breath and whispered.

"You are going to relax your body. You will relax your body.

Your body is relaxing. Your body is relaxed."

The caterpillar's body untangled as he

stretched out on the cool grass.

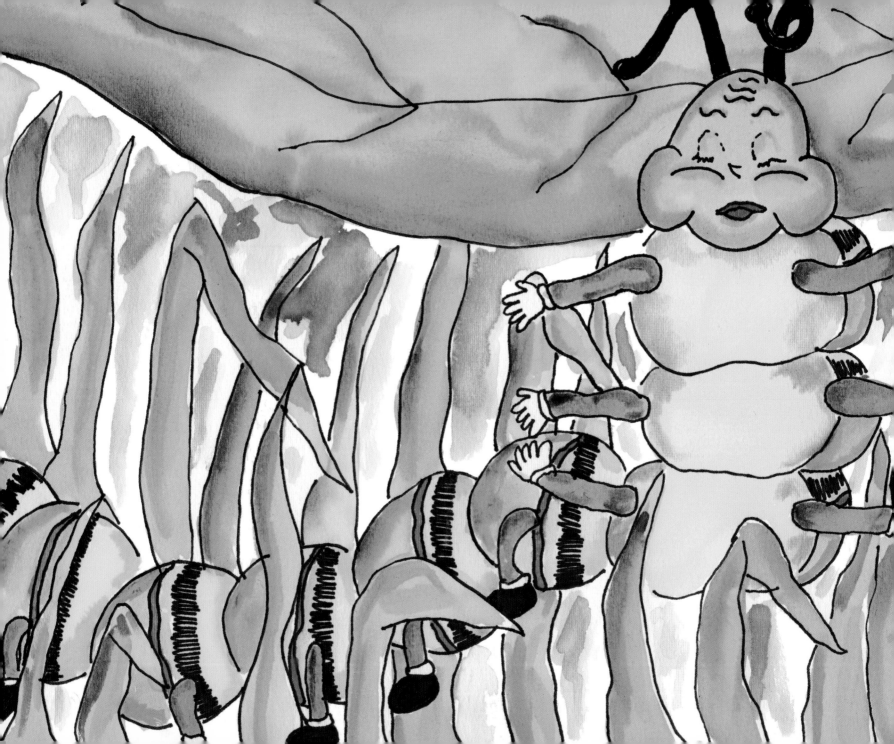

The child spoke slowly.

"You are going to relax your arms.

You will relax your arms. Your arms are relaxing.

Your arms are relaxed."

The caterpillar's arms began to unfold.

The child continued.

"You are going to relax your face.

You will relax your face.

Your face is relaxing. Your face is relaxed."

The caterpillar felt the muscles in his face soften.

The child spoke slowly.

"You are going to relax your mind.

You will relax your mind.

Your mind is relaxing. Your mind is relaxed."

The caterpillar felt his mind become clear and still.

The caterpillar enjoyed how relaxed his body felt.

He focused on how his breath was filling his belly

with warm air. The world felt peaceful.

The caterpillar stayed very still for the next few moments.

He felt his breath move in and out, touching every cell of his body.

After a few moments, the caterpillar felt ready to open his eyes.

The world looked different to him now. Above his head he could

clearly see plenty of green leaves to eat.

Just above the leaves he noticed a strong stem.

The stem had a gentle curve that created a wonderful,

protected spot for his cocoon.

The caterpillar climbed the stem with great balance.

He began to eat the juicy green leaves.

His nourished body grew plumper with each bite.

He felt strong and healthy. The caterpillar was confident

that he could accomplish what he had set out to do.

The caterpillar anchored himself to the stem.

With ease and grace, he began to encase himself in a warm, silky cocoon. The sun filled the cocoon with pure white light.

The cocoon felt soft and safe.

The caterpillar thanked the child with a wink, and said, "goodnight." They both knew that tomorrow would bring wonderful adventures for each of them.